Bitcoin:

The Definitive Guide To Bitcoin Mastery

Jacob Spencer

© Copyright 2017 by Jacob Spencer

All rights reserved.

The following eBook is reproduced below with the goal of providing information that is as accurate and reliable as possible. Regardless, purchasing this eBook can be seen as consent to the fact that both the publisher and the author of this book are in no way experts on the topics discussed within and that any recommendations or suggestions that are made herein are for informational purposes only. Professionals should be consulted as needed prior to undertaking any of the action endorsed herein.

This declaration is deemed fair and valid by both the American Bar Association and the Committee of Publishers Association and is legally binding throughout the United States.

Furthermore, the transmission, duplication or reproduction of any of the following work including specific information will be considered an illegal act irrespective of if it is done electronically or in print. This extends to creating a secondary or tertiary copy of the work or a recorded copy and is only allowed with express written consent from the Publisher. All additional right reserved.

The information in the following pages is broadly considered to be a truthful and accurate account of facts and as such any inattention, use or misuse of the information in question by the reader will render any resulting actions solely under their purview. There are no scenarios in which the publisher or the original author of this work can be in any fashion deemed liable for any hardship or damages that may befall them after undertaking information described herein.

Additionally, the information in the following pages is intended only for informational purposes and should thus be thought of as universal. As befitting its nature, it is presented without assurance regarding its prolonged validity or interim quality. Trademarks that are mentioned are done without written consent and can in no way be considered an endorsement from the trademark holder.

Table of Contents

Introduction 4

Chapter 1: What is Bitcoin 6

Chapter 2: How Bitcoin Works 13

Chapter 3: Bitcoin Valuation 20

Chapter 4: Investing in Bitcoin 22

Chapter 5: Bitcoin: News and Major Corporations 39

Chapter 6: The Future of Bitcoin 42

Conclusion 47

Introduction

Congratulations on downloading *Bitcoin: The Definitive Guide to Bitcoin Mastery* and thank you for doing so. If you were looking for a book that comprehensively covers both the basic and deeper concepts of Bitcoin, then you have purchased the right book!

The chapters in this eBook will begin with the very basic concepts of Bitcoin and explore the origins of Bitcoin itself. After covering the basics, the chapters of this eBook will then explore Bitcoin in greater detail: outlining how the system works and its effects on the current banking system. Bitcoin is a technology that has greatly influenced the personal finances of many, and it very well may continue to do so in the future.

Bitcoin: The Definitive Guide to Bitcoin Mastery will explore the major companies and corporations that were the first to accept Bitcoin as a major form of currency, as these companies played a major role in Bitcoin's progression to being one of the largest forms of cryptocurrency on the digital market.

This eBook will also discuss the pros and cons of viewing Bitcoin as an investment opportunity, outlining the major points of consideration brought to light by some leading experts in the cryptography field.

After learning about the origins and current influence of Bitcoin, the final chapter in this book will look into the future to see how Bitcoin may continue to influence financial institutions and marketplaces for years to come. The final chapter that discusses the future of Bitcoin will include quotes from experts in fields relating directly to Bitcoin and cryptography.

So, whether you are looking into approaching Bitcoin as a serious investment opportunity or if you were just considering a back-up form of payment for sales or services globally, we hope this book will be able to help you not only how Bitcoin works but also its greater influence on private and public financial institutions.

Chapter 1: What is Bitcoin

While Bitcoin has been a digital currency that has been surprisingly fast growing, only an estimated 24% of people in 2015 knew what Bitcoin was. Bitcoin itself is a self-stabilizing economy that relies on blockchain technology and is completely digital. We will get into how Bitcoin and the relating technology works, but only after we cover a brief explanation of what Bitcoin is and what makes the concept so unique.

So, what is Bitcoin? Simply put: Bitcoin is a global currency and a cryptocurrency. While this description may be enough for some, the given description leads most to have two follow up questions: what is a global currency and what is a cryptocurrency? To properly describe Bitcoin, we will begin by defining both terms separately as they relate to the technology that is Bitcoin.

Bitcoin as A Global Currency

Bitcoin can accurately be described as an existing type of global currency because it is able to be used in its current form anywhere around the world. Bitcoin can be used in any country, and transferred to another person across the globe in order to purchase a good or service.

If Person A is in the United States and purchases something from Person B (who is in Japan) using Bitcoin, the currency would not need to be converted from the U.S. Dollar to yen to make the purchase: Person A can send Bitcoin to Person B, who can use the same Bitcoin for other purchases either locally or globally. Bitcoin's use as a globally currency is arguably one of its best qualities: because it can be used anywhere at any time, it does not need first to be converted from the euro to the U.S. dollar to yen. Bitcoin is able to be used to purchase goods and services anywhere by anyone!

Bitcoin can not only be considered a global currency but also a completely independent form of currency as well. Bitcoin is not controlled by any private or government systems. When the concept for Bitcoin was originally introduced, it came with it an algorithm that was created by Bitcoin's founder (or possibly founders) that figures out how many Bitcoins are to be produced each year.

This algorithm ensures that the economy of Bitcoin remains stable, by not releasing too many at once and depreciating their value (or inversely allowing too few Bitcoin to be available, making them a scarcity).

Bitcoin as A Cryptocurrency

A cryptocurrency can be best described as a digital currency that is kept secure by the art of cryptography (which makes codes unsolvable without a specific given key). Because Bitcoin is completely digital, rather than a tangible form of currency which you can store in a bank or wallet, it is categorized by the United States Treasury Department as a "decentralized virtual currency".

The code encryption of cryptocurrencies both regulates and verifies the currency being used in each individual transaction without the need to include a central bank, thus saving time. Banks often hold personal written checks to verify funds anywhere between three to seven days before the funds are available in your account, however by skipping the middleman of a bank the average Bitcoin transaction is able to be reduced to about ten minutes (often less time, but sometimes up to an hour depending on servers and blockchain software).

Thousands of years ago, chickens, cows, and other livestock were barter as currency between small groups of individuals. Over time, urbanization and modernization started to occur and physical currencies of the type we are all familiar with started to appear on the scene. This physical currency is created by a central government and, at least theoretically backed by either silver or gold as well.

The extremely rapid expansion of the internet has led to the need for cryptocurrencies which use complex codes and current exchange rates to determine what a give cryptocurrency is worth.

Cryptocurrencies can also be considered completely self-contained and easy to control, inherently being limited based on blockchain technology. There is theoretically no limit to the amount of value that one unit of a given cryptocurrency could be worth, after all, Bitcoin started off being worth about $.02 and now it is worth about $5,000 as of Sept. 2017.

Decentralized currencies are known to use several different types of verification methods when it comes to validating transactions. The most common of these is the proof of work scheme. Other verification systems include the consensus platform and the consensus protocol.

Despite the fact that Bitcoin is the first successful cryptocurrency to grab the public's attention, doesn't mean that it is the only game in town. In fact, there are currently more than 1,000 different cryptocurrencies on the market today, with a total market cap for all of them ending up near $60 billion. Each of these cryptocurrencies is sure to provide unique weaknesses, but also strengths in hopes of taking the title of the cryptocurrency king from Bitcoin once and for all.

As an example, Litecoin provides confirmation times that are much shorter than Bitcoins and also offers the ability to create decentralized virtual machines like the Ethereum platform. As such, before you start interacting in the marketplace then you are going to want to do your homework and ensure that you are making the best decisions possible.

Cryptocurrency price: Despite the fact that cryptocurrencies like Bitcoin don't have anything holding them back when it comes to their current price, this doesn't mean they don't have various ways to reflect the perceived value of the market as a whole. This means that a majority of a given cryptocurrency's price is going to be determined by its level of available supply versus the demand of the market.

There is more to price than this old adage, however, as external factors play a role as well. Traders who tend to make money through speculation are also known to play significant roles. These are individuals who make an effort to buy up as much of a given cryptocurrency as possible and then hold for as long as they can in hopes of turning a profit. This, in turn, often causes the price to rise to greater heights than pure supply and demand would dictate. This can also lead to negative outcomes such as when many traders start selling off a given currency at once, which will push the price down regardless of what other factors may be in play.

Media support: It doesn't matter what form it comes in, positive press coverage is always going to make a specific cryptocurrency look more successful which, logically, affects the price as well. The media typically takes notice when a new feature is added to an exchange or the underlying blockchain code is tweaked. The media can also take notice in negative situations but, unless the message is that the cryptocurrency is no longer worth any money then it will still cause people to jump on it in hopes of finding a good deal.

The reason for this is that these sorts of stories show the public that Bitcoin and blockchain are still a going concern which makes them appear to be a good investment at a reasonable. This will continue until enough people find out about them that the price becomes disproportionately high. By making sure these types of events make it to the media than those with a vested interest in the currency can help to adjust the dynamic of the price, typically for the better.

Public support: When it comes to creating a successful cryptocurrency, it is important to have not only an active user base, but a loyal fan base as well. This type of public PR team will make it easier for those who are currently on the fence to come down on your side. This is why the most effective cryptocurrencies seem to have the strongest core group of devoted fans. Aside from building trust, diehard supporters typically help with development, generate feedback that is actually useful, and invest their own money back into the platform. Piling up a core of dedicated users will allow the cryptocurrency to create a type of snowball effect, increasing the number of users as it rolls along.

Bitcoin History

Chapter 1 of this book explored what Bitcoin was and its basic features, while chapter 2 explained the basic framework of how Bitcoin works. But where did Bitcoin come from? Where did it originate? Who created Bitcoin and what were the steps in making it one of the most used cryptocurrencies today?

(2007) The first written evidence of Bitcoin's origins appeared in 2007 by the name Satoshi Nakamoto. This identity has never been able to be verified as one person, and is theorized to be a pseudonym for a group of people who created the concept for Bitcoin together collectively.

(8/15/2008) On August 15, 2008 an encryption patent was filed by three individuals: Neal King, Vladimir Oksman, and Charles Bry. All three individuals who applied for the encryption patent were later questioned and deny knowing the real identity of Satoshi Nakamoto.

(8/18/2008) On August 18, 2008 the domain name Bitcoin.org was registered at anonymousspeech.com. Anonymousspeech.com is a website which allows users to send emails while keeping the ability to remain completely anonymous. This website does not offer to sell users' personal registration information to private parties or foreign governments.

(8/31/2008) Satoshi Nakamoto (the rumored original creator of Bitcoin) published a paper on August 31, 2008 that described the Bitcoin currency and its relevance to the prevention of double spending where digital currency is concerned. Double spending is a situation or scheme in which the same set of currency (in this case digital currency) is used to complete two different transactions or purchases. An example of double spending would be if you had $100 in your checking account, and wrote two separate checks for $100 each at the same time to purchase two separate items. The first recipient to deposit the check would receive the $100 payment, but due to double spending the second recipient would be denied payment because the money in your account was already spoken for by the first check that was issued for that amount. Bitcoin prevents double spending by verifying the purchases before they are approved and recorded, so each set of digital currency can only be used for a single purchase.

(1/9/2009) In January of 2009, Bitcoin's original version 0.1 was released.

(1/12/2009) The first Bitcoin transaction took place on January 12, 2009 and was recorded as part of block 170. This transaction took place between Satoshi Nakamoto and Hal Finney, Finney is a cryptography artist.

(5/22/2010) In May of 2010, the first "real world" Bitcoin transaction occurred when Laszlo Hanyecz paid $10,000 Bitcoins (equivalent to $25 USD) to order two large pizzas.

Chapter 2: How Bitcoin Works

Now that we have established basic knowledge that Bitcoin is a digital currency that can be used globally, the next question is how does it work? How can a form of currency that is not printed or tangible be used in any number of transactions across all the world's continents? There is no simple way to answer this question due to the fact that Bitcoin itself relies on blockchain technology in order to be run and stabilized efficiently.

To accurately answer the question of how Bitcoin works, we first need to explore what blockchain technology is. After we have a basic understanding of the technology, we can then dive into some more concepts of Bitcoin's functions such as Bitcoin Wallet and Bitcoin Mining.

Blockchain Technology

When Person A transfers funds using Bitcoin to Person B, the funds are verified and transferred. The transaction is then recorded on a list of recently made transactions through blockchain technology. Once there are a set number of transactions made and recorded, this set of transactions is grouped together as a single "block" and made viewable on the public ledger. Each of these "blocks" of individual Bitcoin transactions begin to form a "chain", hence the given name for the organized technology.

Blockchain technology is largely responsible for Bitcoin's ability to be a secure and anonymous form of digital payment around the world. Blockchain is a public database that anyone can easily view the previously made transactions at any time. Because blockchain is a viewable as a public database, all of the transactions can then be considered permanent.

This means that no one can delete transactions or "rewrite" the ledger in order to suit their personal needs. Blockchain technology does not display the individual's name or other personal information in its public ledger, instead it simply uses account numbers to represent the transactions while simultaneously recording the transaction amount, date, and time.

Cutting Out the Middleman

Another benefit of Bitcoin that many users love is that it is a true "peer to peer" form of payment. Because Bitcoin is not regulated by a government or banking institution it has essentially cut out the middleman, thus making it a true peer to peer payment system and allowing the transfer of funds to process faster. By removing the middleman of a private corporation, banking institution, or government; this setup has also removed some of the room for error when transferring funds during each transaction.

This removal of the middleman also means the transfer of power from the government to private parties. The government uses the economy as a form of control over the country, but they are unable to do this unless the money is put into banking institutions that are federally controlled and regulated.

Theoretically, if all of the money people held was moved into Bitcoin then the people would have all the power. Since the money would be held by individuals and only transferred directly to other individuals, the federal government then loses a portion of control that was in place because of the country's economic framework. Recognizing this potential loss of power, several countries have banned the use of Bitcoin and other forms of digital or cryptocurrency in the past.

Countries That Have "Banned" Cryptocurrencies

Bangladesh: In September 2014, a representative of the Bangladesh government issued an official statement to the public that digital currencies (and Bitcoin in particular) were illegal due to the Anti-Money Laundering regulations already in place by the government. Upon being interviewed about the severity of using digital currencies, an official bank representative stated that the crime of using cryptocurrencies could result in twelve years in prison.

Thailand: In 2013, the Bank of Thailand stated that using Bitcoin had been deemed as an "illegal" practice, though many companies in Thailand still use cryptocurrencies and Bitcoin in particular.

* Ecuador: In 2015 Ecuador was still in the process of building up a national electronic cash system, so the national government "banned" cryptocurrencies to protect the new currency from the benefits offered by a decentralized currency.

Iceland: In March 2014, the Central Bank of Iceland released that served to remind its citizens that the act of purchasing digital currencies was in violation of the Icelandic Foreign Exchange Act which effectively prohibits all Icelandic currency from leaving the country.

* Vietnam: Vietnam banned Bitcoin for use by any existing credit institution in February 2014. The statement released explaining this decision cited two main reasons: the first being that Bitcoin's value fluctuated too much, making it too high an investment risk for credit institutions to take part in. The second reason cited for the ban was that Bitcoin's anonymity made it too easy to be used in criminal transactions. While credit institutions were banned from taking part in Bitcoin transactions, digital currency was not generally banned for personal use.

Ease of Exchange

Bitcoin is a global currency because it can be transferred around the world to any number of people, and they can use the same Bitcoin amount to purchase other goods or services far from where the money originated. The way the Bitcoin system is set up, it makes exchanging currency irrelevant which is especially convenient when transferring funds internationally.

Take for example an individual with $100 worth of Bitcoin traveling from the US to Greece. Normally, the vacationing individual would have to exchange his $100 U.S. dollars for Euros in order to make purchases on vacation. The great convenience with Bitcoin is that there is no longer a need to exchange currency when travelling.

Assuming the country and businesses in question accept Bitcoin: you could travel to anywhere in the world, make your purchases with your Bitcoin balance, and return home without having to exchange currency a single time. For transferring funds between two international individuals: Person A could load $100 of yen from their private bank account to their Bitcoin wallet, and use that money to purchase a product from Person B. Person B (who may live in Italy) can then transfer the $100 worth of Bitcoin received from Person A to their private bank account, automatically exchanging it to be $100 in euros.

If digital and cryptocurrencies were major forms of payment accepted around the world, there would no longer be a need to worry about exchanging currency before being able to make a purchase or being able to have received usable payment for an item you sold. Digital currency apps do the currency exchange automatically when the funds are moved to your bank account, or you could always simply leave them as part of your available Bitcoin balance to be used in future purchases and transactions.

Bitcoin Wallet

Bitcoin Wallet is an application for mobile devices features malware protection since the program itself is only for cellular phones and other mobile devices. Bitcoin Wallet is a fast and reliable digital wallet that prioritizes security by remaining decentralized. Due to the absence of a third party, no private party can lose or freeze available Bitcoin funds in your account which means you are solely in charge of your funds.

This mobile application is extremely user friendly which makes it a great option for anyone interested in Bitcoin that is not so tech savvy. Though Bitcoin wallet does view financial security as a top priority, it is still extremely important to backup your digital wallet and encrypt your mobile device in order to eliminate the risk of theft of your Bitcoin funds. Another benefit of the mobile application Bitcoin Wallet is that the app automatically rotates addresses, making it difficult for anyone to spy on your Bitcoin balance and transactions.

Bitcoin Mining

Bitcoin mining is the process of adding recorded Bitcoin transactions to blockchain (the public transaction ledger). Bitcoin miners use software programs to solve math problems, and are in exchange rewarded with a certain number of Bitcoins. Bitcoin miners play a vital role in the network stability and security by continuously approving transactions.

Blockchain compared to standard databases

The level of centralization trying to be achieved is the biggest difference between a traditional database and a standardized database. With traditional databases, the servers and nodes are going to be kept as close to one another as possible as a means of minimizing lag. Pieces of the system are only decentralized due to space concerns and great pains are taken to keep latency levels at the lowest point possible.

When it comes to blockchain databases, however, all pretext of caring about lag is tossed out the window in order to create a system that can operate autonomously from anywhere in the world. Information stored on a blockchain is beholden to no country and no master, it is egalitarian in every sense of the word.

When taken in tandem with the fact that the system is also extremely secure and autonomous it is not hard to see how it is a major step forward when it comes to how transactions are actually handled. It also goes to show why some people are already calling it the greatest invention since the internet itself.

Blockchain is also notable for its unique cryptography which allows anyone to view their specific details from the blockchain without opening it up to any potential security hazards. This level of security is a core part of the system and exists due to the way that blocks communicate with one another. After a block has been verified, the blockchain then scans it to ensure that the details that are included in it are then accurate based on what information the chain already had to start.

Only if more than half of all the available nodes agree that a particular set of information is correct will it be added to the chain in question. Basically, what this means is that if someone were to hijack a blockchain then they would need enough nodes to be considered 51 percent of the total blockchain and all of those nodes would then need to change their data at exactly the same time. While this is far from easy, it is certainly not impossible either, however it is far too costly to provide any real benefit so it remains secure.

The information you find in a given block is going to be split between details about the block itself and details about the transactions that are included within it. A majority of this information is going to be about the block itself, and the rest is then sent from node to node ensuring that every node is up to date and that every node has a chance to verify the new data as well.

Chapter 3: Bitcoin Valuation

The Perfect Timing

Bitcoin was introduced right after Lehman Bros collapsed in 2008, and the timing of its release may have played a huge part in its initial success. The 2008 United States financial crisis has been described as the worst economic disaster since the Great Depression in 1929. Lehman Bros Holdings Inc. (a financial services firm) filed for bankruptcy on September 15, 2008.

Before filing for bankruptcy, Lehman Bros was the fourth largest investment bank in the United States at the time, and their filing for bankruptcy was the largest in history. Due to the unsteady state of the economy, followed by Lehman Bros collapse, people were generally anxious about the possibility of true economic recovery.

The economy's uncertain future and the general population's trust in the banking system, offered a perfect time for a digital currency like Bitcoin (which would forego the need to leave banks in control of individual's money) to be introduced to the public market place.

With Bitcoin being a completely digital currency, self-stabilizing system that kept people's account information private and anonymous while leaving third party control out of people's pockets, it is easy to see why many may have been optimistic about and willing to try the newly introduced cryptocurrency.

Bitcoin Theft

While Bitcoin has many features and steps in place to ensure financial security for its users, hacking and theft of Bitcoin is possible and has been an issue in a few instances in the past. Blockchain technology is safe and secure, so theft from the main blockchain database by hackers is not generally the issue.

The root problem for the majority of Bitcoin thefts are because independent Bitcoin platforms have not taken enough safety precautions on their end. Below are provided two separate examples of large scale Bitcoin hacking and theft that were cases of very similar causes: errors in exchange network security, not Bitcoin security.

1) MtGox- In February 2014, MtGox (a major Bitcoin exchange network) lost roughly 750,000 in customer owned Bitcoins, which was worth an estimated $620m. After some investigation, it came to light that MtGox was the victim of malleability fraud, in which hackers were able to move Bitcoins to their private accounts while making the MtGox system think the transfers had failed until they had successfully stolen the 750,000 Bitcoins.

2) Bitfinex- In July 2016, Bitfinex (a major Bitcoin exchange network) was hacked. As a result of this hack, an estimated 120,000 Bitcoins (worth roughly $60m) were stolen. This caused the Bitcoin monetary value to crash for a short period, and Bitfinex had no other choice but to suspend trading.

Chapter 4: Investing in Bitcoin

Bitcoin trading can be a profitable form of investment both for those who have been investing in assets for years, as well as those who are just starting out. The Bitcoin market is known for producing large spreads and ending up highly fragmented as well which means there is definitely profit to be made there if you have the skill to take it. The ability to trade on margin or via arbitrage means the options for turning a profit are diverse and there could easily be something for everyone.

Additionally, Bitcoin has a reputation for extreme volatility which means that prices often move very quickly in every direction. Additionally, the market is prone to bubbles which are created when the price rises to artificial highs, which in turn generates unreasonable demand. The bubble can only sustain itself for so long before it pops and the price drops significantly. Each time a bubble is formed, the hype around Bitcoin builds and the media covers the story feeding the bubble until it bursts and everything starts all over again.

If you compare it to other assets, cryptocurrency has very few barriers to entry. In general, all you really need to do is to procure your Bitcoins and you are ready to go. There are plenty of different exchanges available, more than 100 in all, so there is surely one out there that will meet your particular needs.

Why get into Bitcoin

Truly global currency: Unlike more traditional currencies, Bitcoin isn't flat which means it is in no way tied to the economy or policies of any particular country. As such, it is then prone to react to relevant events worldwide, from the decrease in the valuation of the yuan to the implementation of new capital controls, it is actually difficult to determine just what is going to affect the price as it depends entirely on investor reactions. In fact, increased periods of economic uncertainty have actually led to many of Bitcoin's largest increases. One such event, Cyprus's issues with capital control in 2013, led to the creation of a serious Bitcoin bubble.

No limits: While certain markets have trade limits and so exchanges require that you show a certain level of experience before they let you trade on margin, the Bitcoin market has significantly fewer rules than its contemporaries. This goes for the times at which it can be traded as well, as all of the cryptocurrency exchanges are open 24 hours a day, 7 days a week, making even the forex market look like it is slacking.

Additionally, as the exchanges aren't official or connected in any way, it is possible to regularly find prices for a lower amount on one exchange than you can on the other. When this occurs, making a profit is as easy as buying in one place and selling in another. This is a process called arbitrage, and trading in Bitcoin is a good way to take advantage of its benefits.

Large swings: The greater the volatility of an asset, the more potential that asset has for turning a profit. While it also means the asset has a greater potential for risk, but in finance the two are forever entwined. In fact, Bitcoins are currently considered six times more volatile than any of the stocks on the S&P 500 and five times more volatile than gold. It is made quite a name for itself over the past few years for its frequent large price movements, often exceeding five percent in a single day or more. Some of the smaller cryptocurrencies are even more volatile, swinging up to fifteen 15 percent in a given day. As an investor, you are going to want to be prepared for these swings when they occur so you don't lose more than you need to.

Exchange choosing

Before you can start investing successfully, you are going to need to take some time and find the best exchange for you. As Bitcoin is a purely digital currency, if something were to happen to it on the exchange's servers, or if those servers simply shut down one day, then your cryptocurrency might be gone, quite likely forever. This is why doing your homework in this instance is so incredibly important.

Location, location, location: When it comes to choosing an exchange successfully, you are going to want to make a concentrated effort to choose an exchange in your home country. While this won't be an option for everyone, it is ideal if you can make it happen as it provides you with numerous benefits. First and foremost, depending on your country there may be some level of oversight on your exchange which means that if things do end up going downhill, then you won't be completely without recourse.

Even if things never get that severe, having a local exchange will also make it easier for you to get in contact with customer service both because you won't need to worry about a language barrier and because you will be in the same time zone. Finally, a local exchange will make it easier for you to take advantage of periods of high trading volume because they will occur during normal trading hours.

Even if you are considering local exchanges, it is still important to double check that they deal in your local currency as there is no guarantee that this will be the case. Many exchanges operate on a global paradigm which means there is no telling what primary currencies they will deal in.

Be aware of purchase proclivities: If you haven't already purchased your Bitcoins, then you are going to need to go ahead and do so through your exchange. As there is no centralized authority for such things, there is no telling what type of payment the exchange will take in exchange for the currency, it could be PayPal, wire transfers, cash, credit or a direct deposit from your bank account. It is important to be completely confident in your exchange before you make this decision as making the wrong one could end up with you padding out some fraudsters pockets.

When it comes to being confident in your choice, the first thing you are going to want to do is ensure that you read plenty of reviews from people who have already had dealings with the exchange. While you are going to want to see more positive reviews than negative ones, that doesn't mean you should automatically shy away from an exchange with a few negative reviews.

What you are going to want to be on the lookout for, however, is a pattern to those reviews. If you have 15 bad reviews and they all harp on the same issue then there are pretty good odds that it is something you may want to pay attention to. Overall, the more reviews you can find for your exchange of choices, good and bad, the more likely it is that they are on the level.

Know the fee structure: Each exchange is going to charge a different amount of fees when it comes to making a trade through their service. Some will charge a flat transaction fee and others will charge a percentage based on the number of units of currency that are traded.

Additionally, there is a secondary fee that is given to the Bitcoin platform as payment for use of the blockchain and also split between the person or group of individuals who verify the block. Oftentimes, transaction fees are a voluntary expenditure, though in practice if you don't pay then you are unlikely to see your block verified in a timely fashion. Regardless, these fees are typically lower than the fees that you would pay at a more traditional exchange, even when they are combined together, so it all evens out. It currently costs about $3 to pay for a Bitcoin transaction fee.

The amount that the exchange itself is going to charge is going to vary dramatically which means it is in your best interest to consider the fees you will pay before you choose the exchange you would ultimately move forward with. It is important that you know the average rate and that you choose a company that is right in line with it. While it makes sense not to go with an overpriced exchange, it is also important to not go with a discount exchange as there is likely an ulterior motive to their pricing. They may be a scam, or they may just be trying to increase their volume, either way you are going to want to look for something more reliable.

View the book: Any exchange with an order book worth viewing is going to proudly show it off to the public. An order book is simply a list of all of the transactions that a given exchange makes each day. You should always ask to see the order book before making an investment decision as if you are not allowed to see it then there will likely be a reason why, and it is unlikely to be something you appreciate. The more orders that fill the book, the easier it will be for you to make the trades you are interested in, regardless if you are buying or selling. Comparing the order books of your top choices will make it easier to determine what the local trade volume is overall and which exchange has the lion's share of it.

In addition to the order book, you are going to want to ensure that the exchange in question is transparent in a few other ways as well. Transparency means that the owners of the company don't have anything to hide when it comes to their business model which means they are more likely legitimately on the level. The most transparent exchanges even publicize the address of their cold storage along with details outlining the steps they take to verify their Bitcoin reserves. Additionally, transparent companies are going to go through Bitcoin audits from time to time to show their customers that they currently have the liquidity need to pay all of their debts at a particular point in time.

If you cannot find this level of information from the exchange you are considering then there is a possibility that the exchange is actually fractional. A fractional exchange is dangerous because they only keep enough funds on hand to cover a portion of their overall debt. As such, if there is a run on the exchange then they will be unable to give everyone their money and will likely fold. It goes without saying that you are going to want to avoid fractional exchanges as completely as possible.

How quickly will your transactions go through: As Bitcoin transactions are not verified automatically, there is a lag time with most exchanges between when you place your order and when it is fulfilled. This lag time can vary dramatically which means it is in your best interest to know what to expect when you place an order. Regardless of the length of time that you feel is reasonable to wait, it is vital that you choose an exchange that is going to lock in your rates when you make the trade, not when the transaction is verified. Going with the second instead of the first is going to lead to scenarios where you make a trade that looks good on paper, only to find out that it has soured by the time the transaction goes through. Making a trade without knowing the specifics is never recommended and that goes for cryptocurrency trades as well.

Maintain anonymity: Bitcoin and its underlying blockchain technology are built on the idea of anonymous transactions between individuals and if you do your homework then there is no reason that your exchange should have to call that anonymity into question. Assuming you already own the Bitcoins you are looking to invest then you can get started with most exchanges without having to worry about any type of verification process, leaving you as free to fly under the radar as you like.

Overall level of security: When it comes to choosing the right exchange for you, it is important to understand what kind of security they are working with to ensure that your funds remain as safe as possible when they are in the exchange's hands. The first thing you will want to look at is if the site is HTTP or HTTPS. That extra S means that the site is operating using a security protocol so that you can rest easy knowing that your private information is more likely to remain private. You will also want to ensure that your exchange offers a secondary dual-factor authentication when it comes to logging in to make it more difficult for hackers to steal your money or even your identity.

Bitcoin and China: Studies show that a large percentage of Bitcoin's world trading volume comes out of China. As such, it is important that the up and coming Bitcoin investor understand that the Chinese exchanges are more apt to set the market with the rest of the world just following the leader. The primary reason for this fact is that the financial restrictions surrounding cryptocurrency is much less strict in China than anywhere else in the world. As such, Chinese exchanges can offer leverage, lending and futures options that the other Bitcoin exchanges literally cannot beat. You may also be interested to know that Chinese exchanges do not charge additional fees on top of what the blockchain charges for the transaction.

Exchanges to consider

Bitfinex: This Bitcoin exchange offers more trading volume than all of its competition when it comes to USD. It boasts more than 25,000 Bitcoins traded every single day, seven days a week. It also does not require secondary verification for users who bring their own Bitcoins to the table.

Bitstamp: Known for being one of the oldest continuously running exchanges on the market, this exchange has been around since 2011. It is still the exchange with the second highest degree of overall volume with more than 10,000 Bitcoins being traded every day.

OkCoin: This exchange is unique in that it is based in China but focuses exclusively on USD trades. Functionally, what this means is that users can trade in USD in a market that is far more lenient than they might otherwise be used to.

Coinbase: While it is currently the fourth largest Bitcoin exchange in the US, this exchange was actually the first exchange to open in the US. It typically sees volume greater than 8,000 Bitcoins each day.

Kraken: When it comes to trading in EUR, there is no exchange that boasts a greater level of volume than Kraken, trading more than 6,000 Bitcoins each day. They are also one of the top 15 USD exchanges in the world.

Investment basics to remember

When it comes to investing in Bitcoin, your goal should be to work smarter instead of harder. While you can sit in front of a computer screen all day and trade based on small changes in Bitcoin's price, you will see just as much benefit in the long-term by buying from a point of strength and then adopting a long-term buy and hold strategy.

The amount of volatility that comes along with investing in Bitcoin is so high that taking an active approach to investing in more of a day-trading style is likely to see you put in far more work for an unreliable return. Bitcoin's volatility is so high right now that trading in the short-term does not significantly improve your potential returns overall.

Compounding: One of the key aspects of investing is the concept of compounding. In order to compound your investments, whenever you come upon profit you are going to want to put it right back into the investment itself. Reinvesting your initial returns both early and often can lead to a significant increase in your overall results. If you have at least 20 years left until you can retire, then compounding might just be the most vital tool in your investment toolbox.

As an example, consider the fact that a 25-year-old only needs to save $900 a month in order to be a millionaire by the time they retire at age 60, assuming they see a steady but unimpressive five percent return on their investment per year (remember this is what Bitcoin often moves in a day) for 35 years. However, if that same individual waited just 10 years to start investing then they would need to save about $2,000 each month to hit the same goal in the same period of time. Finally, if they were to wait until they were 45 to start saving then they would need to invest over $4,000 each month to hit their original goal by the time they were 60.

Understand your personal investing habits: There are a million different investing strategies out there because there are a million different ways to invest successful. No strategy is going to be right for everyone and in order to find the one that suits you best you are going to need to understand how comfortable you are with risk. As you are investing in cryptocurrency, you are obviously going to become more comfortable with it - but there are still varying degrees of acceptance, which will affect your ideal investing strategy significantly.

Additionally, it is important that you have clear goals in place when it comes to your investing strategy. This could be something like keeping your initial investment going strong, or it could involve taking maximum risk in order to grow your pile of Bitcoins as quickly as possible. Based on your goals, you may even want to split your investment fund and invest differently to reach differing goals. It doesn't matter what your specific plans are, as long as you take the time to clearly identify what those plans are. It is important that you also keep in mind that your goals are not going to exist in a vacuum which means it is helpful to factor in external factors when determining what they are as well.

In order to best determine your goals, it is important that you understand how much money you would be comfortable losing, as you should never invest money that you can't afford to lose. It is important to be honest with yourself when it comes to choosing this amount as you will not be able to make rational decisions for the money if you are worried about losing it all of the time.

Remember, risk leads to profit, you literally can't have one without the other. If you have at least 20 years of investing ahead of you then you are naturally going to be able to take more risk, because you will have a longer period of time to recoup your losses then if you were just a few years out of retirement.

Once you know what your acceptable level of risk is, you will also need to think about how comfortable you are going to micromanage your trades. Bitcoin's price definitely moves enough to warrant a closer look, but only if you have the time and energy available to devote to the task. If you aren't sure how much time you are going to have to manage your investments it is generally better to err on the side of caution to ensure you plan works out in the end.

Assuming you are looking for long-term results then you are going to want to go with a buy and hold strategy which will provide you average, if not outstanding returns in the long run. Keep in mind that average returns for cryptocurrencies are going to be much higher than with other assets due to the level of volatility in play.

Finally, you are going to want to keep in mind how much you know about Bitcoin and how comfortable you are going to be when it comes time to make decisions regarding your investments. Ideally, you will want your investment decisions to be based around plenty of research and a general understanding of the market as a whole. While you don't need to know everything, you definitely need to know enough to know what you don't know.

It is also especially important that you never let yourself be talked into any types of investment that you haven't researched personally, regardless of how much of a sure thing the other party assures you it is. When it comes to investing successfully it is always better to be safe than sorry.

Diversify: While starting with cryptocurrency investing with Bitcoin is a logical decision as it is the leader in the market, no matter how strong an individual investment might seem, diversifying your investment into at least two places is always going to be a more reliable choice. Diversifying will help you to more reliably ensure that your investments remain relatively stable if a portion of them takes a sudden loss, which with Bitcoin is a strong possibility. Ultimately you will want to diversify into about five different cryptocurrencies.

Get when the getting is good: If you are looking to take a long-term approach to investing then from time to time you are going to lose some money. While this is unfortunate, it is a part of investing and the sooner you come to terms with it, the better. This is a natural part of the investment process, and if you are in for the long-term then your best course of action will often be to not change horses in midstream and retain your holdings. This will not always be the right choice, however, and if the initial losses are just the opening salvo in a greater chain of losses then this is something you should be aware of. Even if you have taken a very passive approach to investing, you are still going to want to keep your ear to the ground when it comes to news about your holdings.

If the reason for the dip is largely anticipated then you are fine to stay the course, otherwise it might be time to sell. This first loss might just be the tip of the iceberg which means you are going to want to focus on maximizing profit in the short-term instead. Luckily, unlike with other assets, with Bitcoin you will always have the ability to cash out almost immediately which means your potential for loss will generally be minimal as long as you act quickly.

Regardless of the actual situation, it is important to never let emotions come into play when you are dealing with your investments. If you have reason to believe that more losses are on the way then staying the course and wishing that things would turn around is never going to do you any good. If you want to see positive results in the long-term then getting attached to your investments is literally not an option.

Successful investment tips

When you first start investing in Bitcoin, investing will be easy, investing successfully will be much more difficult. What follows is a list of things you will want to keep in mind in order to make the transition from one to the other as smooth as it can possibly be.

Consider Bitcoins like any other commodity: Bitcoin actually has a fair bit in common with other commodities that frequently sees investors. First, it has other uses outside of investments, such as precious or base metals, and second, they are both traded on open market exchanges. Practically, this means when it comes to choosing to invest in companies that are based on the Bitcoin blockchain you are going to want to focus on what the company in question brings to the market as a whole that adds value in the real world. The more difficult it is to answer that question, the less likely you are going to want to invest in that company.

Positive adoption rate: Currently, all of the cryptocurrencies on the market (more than 1,000 in total) can boast a market cap of approximately 60 billion dollars which is more than Tesla and enough to put it in the company of major corporations like Microsoft and Coca Cola. While this is certainly a huge number, and most of it is attributable to Bitcoin, what makes it truly meaningful is that it has been achieved despite the remarkably small number of regular users the cryptocurrency has.

As such, usage in the real world has gone hand in hand with investment prices,which means that it seems unlikely that Bitcoin is going to be going anywhere soon. What this means is that while Bitcoin is undeniably volatile in the short-term, it is consistently proving itself to be a viable long-term investment choice.

These are becoming increasingly important as, regardless of your investment plans, the more people who use Bitcoins on a regular basis, the greater the profit for those who got in early. Even better, despite the fact that each Bitcoin is worth approximately $5,000 as of September 2017, there is still plenty of reason to consider buying in now to be getting in early. Even better, when the market eventually hits a saturation point and Bitcoins become mainstream then its tendency to form bubbles will be nullified and the price will settle into more normal rhythms.

Understand the cycle of all investments: While cryptocurrencies might be different from other types of investments in a lot of ways, Bitcoin has already proven that it is going to stick to the same cycle as any other type of investment. Even the most novice investor is familiar with the "market cycle", which can be loosely defined as - *the pattern that the price of all types of investments eventually go through sooner or later.*

First the market experiences optimism about some type of investment, this then builds into a thrill as the price continues moving upward and everything is great, things eventually peak at a euphoria and a sustained surge of potential investors which the market cannot sustain forever. Once this occurs, the investment drops in price during a bout of anxiety, sees a small resurgence during a period of denial then steadily decrease during periods of market fear and depression before those who have been holding out panic and sell off their holdings at last. From there, things eventually get moving again and panic turns back into depression and then prices start to increase as hope returns, followed by relief and then returning to optimism.

Bitcoin has already completed the full cycle more than once, most recently bottoming out in 2014 and currently on its way past optimism. The euphoria period is still likely years away so there is still plenty of time for those who are interested in investing to still get in on a reasonable share of the profits. The euphoria stage is likely not going to hit critical mass for about five years which is about the time needed for the adoption of blockchain technology, along with Bitcoin and other cryptocurrencies, to truly become mainstream.

While this certainly makes it an exciting time to be investing in Bitcoin, it is important to keep in mind that much like the dotcom boom in the late 90s, more than 80 percent of all the cryptocurrencies on the market won't survive to see the promised land. While Bitcoin has its legacy on its side, there are several aspects of it that are somewhat limited in scope for what it has become and many other blockchains, with Ethereum in the lead, are already doing most, if not all, of what Bitcoin does but better, faster, and often, cheaper. Just because it was the first, doesn't mean it will stand the test of time.

Try and remain abreast of the next big thing, and don't be afraid to shift your investments if the time comes that the move makes sense. Remember, you can't be emotional if you want to make profitable investments.

Understand Ethereum

While Bitcoin is the only cryptocurrency that a majority of Americans can name, it is far from what could be considered an up and comer. While Bitcoin is a solid investment choice in the moment, when it comes times to diversify your portfolio then Ethereum is most definitely the second-best choice.

Ethereum has currently seen about 50 percent of the transactions blockchain has, despite only having been around for about three years.

Additionally, if you look at standard transaction chart, you will see that Bitcoin's price has seen a large number of peaks and valleys over the years. On the contrary, the Ethereum blockchain has remained relatively bullish since a security issue forced a major fork in the underlying blockchain. Cryptocurrencies are social in nature which means that the more new users continue to flock towards Ethereum the greater its utility, and therefore it value, will do the same.

This means it is worth paying attention to for several reasons, the first of which is that the blockchain that Bitcoin is based on is already running at maximum capacity. It can typically process roughly seven transactions each second, which sounds fast until you realize there are currently nearly four million transactions waiting to be approved by the chain at any given time. This means that even if the blockchain stopped accepting new transactions right now, it would still take about a week to make it through the backlog. Right now, the code that supports the Bitcoin blockchain simply can't keep up with its demand.

Furthermore, while smart contracts were discovered using the Bitcoin blockchain, the Ethereum blockchain makes them much easier to develop, to the point where the Ethereum platform has created an entire virtual machine to create apps that deal with them. While relatively few of these projects have come online just yet, as they do the platform will likely experience an even greater spike of new users.

Chapter 5: Bitcoin: News and Major Corporations

Funding Wikileaks

One large and well-known organization that relies on Bitcoin in order to accept and process donations is Wikileaks. Wikileaks is a global and nonprofit organization that specializes in the verification and publication of secret information obtained from anonymous sources. In late 2010 (November), WikiLeaks released secret U.S. diplomatic cables.

The result from the release of this information was that their donations were then blocked by the Bank of America, Visa, MasterCard, Western Union, and PayPal. While these private companies have the right to refuse service to any one person or organization the block of donations was no doubt a result of pressure from the United States government after the release of sensitive information to the public. Wikileaks then turned to Bitcoin as an option for receiving financial donations, soon after turning to Bitcoin wiki leaks received upwards of $32,000 from over 1100 separate Bitcoin donations. Wikileaks still relies on Bitcoin in order to receive anonymous monetary donations from people every day.

Black Market Purchases

Another known website that has relied heavily on Bitcoin and greatly influenced its value temporarily is Silk Road. Silk Road was an online website that could only be accessed through the dark web, which users needed to purchase specialized software in order to access. After you were able to gain access to the Silk Road website you could purchase anything from drugs to passports, hire anyone from assassins to computer hackers. Silk Road's method of accepted payment was Bitcoin, largely because it allowed its customers to purchase contraband items while remaining anonymous. Over two years the website Silk Road generated 9.5 million Bitcoins which was over $1.3 billion in revenue and had over 950,000 users for the website.

As Silk Road's popularity grew, Bitcoin became more and more well-known for being used to enable illegal activity, which then continued to raise government interest. In October 2013, the United States government shut down the Silk Road website. Due to the shutdown of Silk Road, Bitcoin's volume rose, while the monetary price of Bitcoin temporarily took a dive and then quickly recovered to be valued at more than it was before the government shut down Silk Road. When the Silk Road website was shut down the FBI arrested Ross William Ulbricht, who was the site's original creator and charged him with drug trafficking, money laundering, and computer hacking.

Major Business and Bitcoin

The following major businesses accept Bitcoin as a valid form of payment for goods and services: Subway, Microsoft (in both Xbox and Windows store), Gyft (Gift card purchases), and the Libertarian Party (a political party recognized in the United

States of America). With these major businesses, corporations, and parties accepting Bitcoin as valid payment; it is entirely possible that Bitcoin will continue to be used by more and more people globally as a preferred payment method.

Chapter 6: The Future of Bitcoin

Fedcoin: The United States is currently actively looking for ways to make Bitcoin less appealing to criminals who are looking to launder their money, among other things, without sacrificing their utility and security in the process. Analysts in Washington DC seem to think that the federal govern is currently formulating plans to surpass Bitcoin by implanting what is tentatively being called Fedcoin. By creating its own blockchain it not only solves the problems it is looking to solve, but also turns a profit on the backend as well. The idea here is that the Federal Reserve could turn its resources to creating a federal blockchain fairly easily, once that is done, the genesis block will be created and then Fedcoins will be available to purchase at the rate of $1 per, for a time at least.

The Fedcoin will operate in just the same way as Bitcoin, except that one user, the federal reserve, would have the ability to destroy or create new blocks at will, theoretically meaning it could target blocks that it had reason to suspect of black market dealings directly. The Reserve would also have the power to fork the chain if it were hacked and adjust the rate that miners would be paid. Essentially, it would be a hybrid cryptocurrency, one that is decentralized for personal transactions and centralized enough to give control of supply to a single entity and erase the idea of anonymous transactions completely.

While this may sound a bit like a dystopian conspiracy theory, it is unfortunately, much closer to reality than you might expect. Last fall, Bitcoin authorities met at the Federal Reserve for a restricted meeting that was attended by Janet Yellen, the Federal Reserve Chair, herself. Attendees also included representatives from the Bank for International Settlements, the World Bank, International Monetary Fund, to name a few.

While publicly, the meeting was supposed to discuss utilizing blockchain when it comes to improving transactions between banks, insiders believe that Fedcoin was discussed in detail as well. In fact, the owner of a company named Chain, which is in the blockchain business, even gave a speech with the title "Why Central Banks will Issue Digital Currencies" in which he recommends getting into the game sooner than later.

One of the biggest reasons that the Federal Reserve wants to move forward is its stated desire to stabilize the idea of cryptocurrency through a direct connection with more traditional capital. This link will likely be mandatory either, at least after leaving a window open for early adopters. When Fedcoin comes into existence you will likely find legal tender harder and harder to come by.

Russia: Russia has seen a big turn when it comes to its stance on Bitcoin. This year has seen them legalize the use of cryptocurrency, after previously having a law in place that said the use of cryptocurrency was good enough for a jail sentence. This abrupt policy shift comes from Russia's ongoing monetary troubles. It has had issues with decreasing oil price combined with foreign sanctions that make foreign investors few and far between. These issues have increased the costs of accessing money which has hurt the banking sector significantly.

During this same period, the country has also seen an extreme increase in corruption in the banking sector, specifically local banks removing money from the country through money laundering endeavors. Since 2014, more than 100 banks have closed, and many more are expected to close before 2019. Perhaps unsurprisingly, this has proved to be a serious drain on the country, costing it more than $50 billion at last count. This ongoing battle has also shed light on concerns regarding overall liquidity for the country and its Central Bank which explains its change in stance when it comes to cryptocurrency.

The logic here is that if Russian citizens have access to other forms of banking then it is less likely that they will add additional strain to the current system. Even better, the improved focus on digital currencies would decrease the power of the regional bank administrators by reducing the importance of their interpersonal relationships and hopefully weeding out some corruption. Currently the banking structure in Russia is so hard to muddle through that the smaller banks essentially operate unilaterally.

In order to cut all of the fraud off at the source, the Russian government is working to create several technical applications that will make it easier for them to identify real time transactions. Russia isn't looking to create its own type of Fedcoin, rather, they are working to build their own blockchain to take advantage of its digital ledger. It is currently unclear exactly what plans Russia has for blockchain technology or if those in Moscow are going to be supportive of the plans. Given the recently rectified stance against Bitcoin, however, it is likely that movement in this direction will be supported.

China: China is at the forefront of cryptocurrency in this instance as well, having already announced in June 2017 that the People's Bank have already created a digital currency that can seamlessly scale based on load. While all the details have yet to be finalized, the information that has been released thus far shows that the bank is looking to release the cryptocurrency the same time it does the renminbi, while no true timetable for doing so has been found. The new cryptocurrency has also already been tested via transactions with the country's commercial banks and the People's bank.

This marks a new benchmark for cryptocurrencies as a whole and will only serve to help solidify blockchain's legitimacy to much of the world. It also shows that China is committed to discovering the economic, logistical and technical challenges that come along with the development of a true digital currency. It is also likely to have serious ramifications for the world economy as a whole. This is the case as a digital fiat currency is essentially as good as a banknote which would decrease the transaction costs of a variety of financial transactions significantly. That, in turn, would make these types of services much more affordable to the masses who do not have access to them currently.

While giving millions of its citizens access to services they have never had before is nice, there is a fair chance that the Chinese government is also excited by the fact that releasing their cryptocurrency will give them extended control when it comes to the cryptocurrency market which has taken off in the country in a big way. A centralized digital currency will also be much easier to track which means it can help the government to crack down on corruption at the same time.

The cryptocurrency will also allow for an easier look into the current status of local economies as well. It will also make it easier to introduce the renminbi to the world as a currency they should care about as it will be much easier to deal with digitally than it would using current conditions. Other countries are already paying attention to China's new project because of the way it is predicted to interact with the central banking system. It is said to generate wallets for those who have an account at the bank that makes it easy to set up a cryptocurrency account aside from your traditional account.

It is also noteworthy as it doesn't seem to be based on the traditional Bitcoin blockchain like 95 percent of all other cryptocurrencies. Instead, it utilizes a distributed ledger in a limited format to prevent bottlenecks when the number of transactions increases dramatically. Rather, it gains access to the digital ledger only when it needs to update its records or to check if an individual has been holding onto certain funds for a prolonged period of time.

Conclusion

Thank you for making it through to the end of *Bitcoin: The Definitive Guide to Bitcoin Mastery*, let's hope it was informative and able to provide you with all of the tools you need to achieve your goals, whatever it is that they may be. Just because you've finished this book doesn't mean there is nothing left to learn on the topic, expanding your horizons is the only way to find the mastery you seek. Bitcoin is the flagship for all of cryptocurrency and it is at the forefront of a tumultuous industry. Even if you read everything there is to know about Bitcoin, blockchain, or cryptocurrencies today - tomorrow there could very well be new information that puts everything you thought you knew in a new light. The only way to truly stay on top of things is to become a lifelong learner, only then will you truly find the success that you are looking for.

This is truly a time that the history will look back on as the rise of cryptocurrency, and Bitcoin has without a doubt been there to lead the way. It doesn't matter if you are interested in investing in your future with Bitcoins, building a business on blockchain, the technology that Bitcoin popularized, or simply want to use some Bitcoins to make peer-to-peer digital transactions, it is easy to see how Bitcoin's success is only going to improve moving forward.

Understanding this idea and making the most of it are two different things, however, and it is important that you finish reading this book committed to taking advantage of Bitcoin in your own life. Bitcoin is at the forefront of a once in a generation technological advancement and if you let it pass you by, there is a good chance you will regret it later. So, what are you waiting for? Don't let your Bitcoin dreams pass you by, get out there and make them a reality.

www.ingramcontent.com/pod-product-compliance
Lightning Source LLC
Chambersburg PA
CBHW050027230526
45470CB00003B/1165